A Sau

The History of Henderson's Relish

Mark Dawson

British Library Cataloguing in Publication Data: a catalogue entry for this book is available from the British Library.

ISBN 978-1-914408-28-1

Printed and bound in Great Britain by Biddles Books Limited, King's Lynn, Norfolk.

For Nic, Henry and Bess

Contents

List of Illustrations   p v

Acknowledgements   p vi

Notes and Abbreviations   p viii

Introduction   p 1

Chapter 1   p 3

Chapter 2   p 13

Chapter 3   p 18

Chapter 4   p 29

Endnotes   p 39

Timeline   p 45

Index   p 46

List of Illustrations

Figure 1. St Mary Magdalene's Church, Walkeringham p 4

Figure 2. The entrance to Green Lane Works p 8

Figure 3. Henry Henderson's grave p 12

Figure 4. The Shaw family p 14

Figure 5. The site of the first factory p 17

Figure 6. Flyer issued by Hendersons Relish Limited p 19

Figure 7. Charles Hinksman p 21

Figure 8. Hendersons factory at 41 Leavygreave Road p 26

Figure 9. Hendersons current factory p 31

Figure 10. Dr Kenneth Freeman p 33

Acknowledgements

In April 2019, I gave a short talk on the history of Henderson's Relish to the Leeds Symposium on Food History and Traditions. By chance someone in the audience at that talk also attended the Malton Food Lovers Festival a month later and mentioned it to Matt Davies, general manager of Hendersons (Sheffield) Ltd, who was at the festival with their stall. Matt contacted me and generously invited me over to the factory to meet him and managing director Pamela Freeman and her daughter, Julia Waxman, to see what additional information they could provide. I was given access to Hendersons own historical records: wages books, minute books, accumulated press cuttings and some mid-twentieth century notes on production costs. With these I was able to turn the short talk into this short book and for that I thank Matt, Pamela and Julia as well as the anonymous symposiast.

I confess to being a fan of Hendo's. It is a fine brew, as someone else has said. As a food historian, however, I find the history of Henderson's Relish fascinating. It is a remarkable story, one that I think is worth telling and one that I hope people will enjoy reading.

Mark Dawson, Chesterfield, March 2021

Notes and Abbreviations

Currency, Weights and Measures

Values are given in pre-decimal currency and Imperial weights and measures.

1 d = 1 penny

1 s = 1 shilling (12 pence)

£1 = 1 pound (20 shillings or 240 pence)

1 fl. oz = 1 fluid ounce (approx. 30 ml)

1 pint = 20 fluid ounces (approx. 568 ml)

1 gallon = 8 pints (approx. 4.5 litres)

What's in a name?

Henderson's Relish (or Hendo's) is always spelled with an apostrophe.

The company name, Hendersons Relish Limited or Hendersons (Sheffield) Limited, has no apostrophe.

A note on sources (or should that be sauces?)

I was able to greatly expand the scope of my initial paper on Henderson's Relish thanks to the material kept by Hendersons (Sheffield) Limited themselves and which I was shown by Matt Davies. None of these records are catalogued and so I will provide a note on them here and how I have referred to them in the text and endnotes.

Hendersons Minute Books

There are two volumes of compiled minutes from board meetings of Hendersons Relish Limited and Hendersons (Sheffield) Limited. Many of the entries were typed and then pasted into the books. Some additional items (such as the flyer produced by the company in 1940) were also pasted into these books. The first volume contains minutes from meetings from 1940 to 1972. The second volume contains minutes from meetings from 1972 to 2008.

Hendersons Wages Books

Hendersons was never a big company and wages were recorded in a variety of different types and formats of wages books, presumably obtained from commercial stationers. Each book covers a single financial year. Interestingly, separate wages books for the relish factory in Sheffield were kept during the period of Shaws ownership and the wages books are one of the few sources of information on the company from that time (on enquiry, Shaws themselves stated they had no records). The wages books run from the early 1910s through to the 1980s, although not all years survive.

Other records

The company has scrapbooks with newspaper cuttings, preserved it seems with the sense of pride one gets in the achievements of one's offspring. There is also a notebook, which was used on several separate occasions in the 1930s, the 1950s and the 1960s for recording the costs and profits of producing 25 gallons of relish (probably by Charles Hinksman and Neville Freeman). I hasten to add that this notebook does not contain the secret recipe for making Henderson's Relish, but together with the information from the minute books and wages books it helped me put together some estimates for just how much relish was being produced at those dates.

Introduction

Henderson's Relish is a Sheffield phenomenon. Beloved in its native city, Henderson's Relish or Hendo's is often unknown and hard to find outside of it. This is something which the company that makes it is trying to change, but which is familiar to generations of Sheffielders who've found that their own fortune and fame has travelled further than that of their favourite sauce. Nightclub owner and bon viveur Peter Stringfellow was drawn to the bright lights of London in the 1970s, but his usual fry-up to recover from the night before just wasn't the same without a dash of Henderson's. None of the local girls he met had heard of it and he made sure to stock up when he next went back to Sheffield. Actor Sean Bean calls Henderson's 'a fine brew' and once bought two gallons on hearing a rumour that the company was about to close. The company has had its up and downs, as will be seen. Two gallons: a lifetime's supply? Probably not considering the way aficionados lash it onto their food. Rick Savage of heavy metal group Def Leppard says the band drove tour managers mad with demands for Henderson's on their meat pies whether they were in Melbourne, Milan, Massachusetts, or Manchester.[1]

So, what does Hendo's taste like? According to Matt Helders of The Arctic Monkeys it's like Worcestershire sauce, only a million times better.[2] Physically, it does resemble Worcestershire sauce, which led to 'Hendogate' in 2014, when Labour MP for Lewisham, Jim Dowd, cited Hendo's as an example of parasitic packaging, believing it to be a rip-off copy of Lea and Perrin's original Worcestershire Sauce. He immediately found himself at the centre of a furore and was obliged to apologise to South Yorkshire relish fans, showing what a good sport he was by visiting Hendersons new factory and helping out on the production line.[3] Indeed, Henderson's has sported the classic orange labels for a century, although ironically early ones did bear the legend 'A Worcester-type sauce'. But passions run high where relish is concerned. Singer Richard Hawley, on return from a nine-month tour of the US bereft of his favourite sauce, burst into tears at a plateful of sausages and mash topped with Hendo's.[4] As Sheffield comedian Tom Wrigglesworth has put it, yes, you can describe Henderson's Relish as Sheffield's answer to Lea & Perrin's; but, for Sheffielders, it's the answer to everything.[5]

Hendo's is inextricably linked to Sheffield. 'Essence of Sheffield', is the title of an artwork by local artist Peter McKee, showing a burly steelworker carefully pouring the black stuff into a characteristic orange-labelled bottle.[6] Hendo's seemingly forged in a crucible at Firth Brown's. It is made today in Sheffield as it always has been, according to a 'secret' formula, handed down over the years and known only to a handful of people – part of its mystique. Yet this essence of Sheffield is not made to some traditional recipe with local ingredients (all listed on the label). Besides water, vinegar, sugar and caramel, Hendo's is flavoured with garlic oil and a trio of exotic Asian spices: tamarinds, cayenne pepper and cloves – none of them native to South Yorkshire. In fact, its originator, Henry Henderson, was from Nottinghamshire. The history of the company, frequently mythologised in the local press, is far from straight forward and is a remarkable survival story. How did this thin, spicy sauce come into being and how has it retained such a firm and largely localised following?

2

Chapter 1

From Nottinghamshire with love

Henry Henderson was born in 1850. His parents ran a farm in Walkeringham, a small village in north Nottinghamshire, a few miles over the River Trent from Gainsborough. It was a large family. Henry was the youngest of eight children listed in the household in the 1851 census and a decade later he had three more, younger siblings. [7] It was a substantial farm, listed variously as between 80 and 110 acres in succeeding censuses and large enough to require a live-in servant to help Henry's father, Joseph, and his mother, Hannah. They probably relied on the older boys to help on the farm as well, because by the 1871 census when only their youngest daughter, Hannah (14), was left at home they had two live-in farm servants. [8]

Joseph Henderson, senior, had been born and lived all his long life on the farm, but his large brood of children would need to go out into the changing world of Victorian Britain to seek their fortune. Henry's eldest brother, Joseph, became a greengrocer in Rotherham and was a regular stallholder at Doncaster market. [9] Henry himself was apprenticed to Robert Brock, miller of Haxey, a few miles to the north in Lincolnshire. [10] Brock was the miller at Low Burnham and the tower of Burnham Mill (formerly known as Brock's Mill) still stands. [11] In his early twenties and probably on completion of his apprenticeship, Henry like his brother moved to South Yorkshire, to the opportunities in the burgeoning industrial city of Sheffield.

Figure 1. St Mary Magdalene's Church, Walkeringham, Nottinghamshire. Henry Henderson was born here in 1850. His parents ran a farm in the village and are buried in the churchyard.

Source. Photograph by the author.

He may have come to Sheffield for work, but Henry Henderson soon found love. In 1874, he married 18-year old Clara Cornthwaite and the couple set up home at Freedom Street, Walkley, on the northern edge of the city.[12] A daughter, Edith, was born in 1875 and by the time of the 1881 census the family had moved to Furnival Street in the city centre.[13]

On his marriage in 1874 and in the 1881 census, Henry was described as a miller, but by the early 1880s he seems to have decided on a change of career. In September 1882, a notice appeared in the *Sheffield Independent* newspaper announcing that the partnership of William Eyre and Henry Henderson, grocers and drysalters, trading as 'Henderson & Eyre', was dissolved by mutual consent and that Henry Henderson would carry on the business from their premises in Earl Street.[14] Exactly when Henderson moved into this new line of business is unclear, but we can speculate as to why. Flour milling was undergoing radical change in the late-nineteenth century. Large rolling mills, mostly located at coastal ports to process imported grain, accounted for the majority of the market.[15] For Henderson, a move to the city and a change of career may have been an escape from grinding poverty, quite literally in his case.

In 1883, Henry Henderson was recorded in the Sheffield trade directories for the first time, described as a wholesale grocer.[16] By this time, he had acquired premises at 44 Green Lane. This was a potentially plum location outside the ornamental factory entrance of Messrs Hoole & Co, which still stands in Sheffield's Kelham Island district – its former industrial heartland next to the River Don. Grocers sold food colourings, spices and preservatives and also a growing range of ready-made pickles and sauces. They would have seen how much these products cost and how much the raw ingredients cost. Some may have done the maths and wondered if they could come up with their own recipe for success.

Recipes for spiced sauces had begun to appear in English cookery books from the turn of the eighteenth century, usually made with either mushrooms, walnuts, oysters or anchovies. One of the earliest was written down by Rebecca Price, who compiled a manuscript collection of recipes from

1681 to 1710 and included a recipe for 'catchup to be put into any sauces'. These 'catchups' were bottled and stored and provided a quick way of introducing flavour to dishes, bypassing the lengthy preparations of French cookery then in vogue amongst the wealthy.[17] The recipes were influenced by the spicy sauces encountered by British merchants in the far east. The term 'catchup' derived from a Chinese (Amoy) dialect word for fish sauce.[18] By the end of the eighteenth century, branded versions of these sauces were starting to be sold commercially. Popular brands were Cock's Reading Sauce, Harvey's Sauce and later and more famously Lea & Perrin's Worcestershire Sauce, first sold in 1837. These sauces were aimed at middle class households who may not have the time, the skilled staff, or the inclination to make their own. Branding also gave a measure of assurance in an age when much food was adulterated.[19]

As the British empire expanded in the nineteenth century, bottled and branded goods went with its servants and soldiers and in return came new recipes, tastes and ingredients, such as tamarind, a sour fruit pulp often added to dishes in south-east Asia to provide an acidic sharpness. Cakes of dried and processed tamarind pulp could be exported easily and cheaply. By the second half of the nineteenth century, a new wave of British branded spicy sauces and relishes were being produced, many of which included tamarind, but omitted anchovies. These include many of the popular British brown sauces that are still manufactured today, such as HP, OK and Daddies.[20] Chief amongst these at the time, however, was Yorkshire Relish marketed by Goodall, Backhouse & Co. In 1837, Leeds chemist, Robert Goodall, started bottling and selling the relish made by his wife. In 1858, Goodall entered partnership with two other chemists, Henry Backhouse and his brother-in-law, William Powell to form Goodall, Backhouse & Co. In 1872, the firm of Goodall, Backhouse & Co. sold 670,000 bottles of Yorkshire Relish. Two years later, they built the then largest factory in the world in Leeds and by 1885 they were selling 8 million bottles a year worldwide.[21]

Sauces like Yorkshire Relish sold not just to the middle class, but to the working class. British agriculture suffered an economic depression in the 1870s and 1880s in the face of cheap food imports, encouraging many like Henry Henderson to look for work in industrial towns and cities. Those in employment in towns and cities, however, found food was cheaper and their wages went further. Surveys from the late-nineteenth and early-twentieth century suggest that in general the poor had enough to eat, although the quality and nutritional value of their food was often inadequate. Starchy, stodgy foods (bread and increasingly potatoes) predominated with cheaper cuts of meat. Cooking facilities were limited in many working-class homes and cheap and filling takeaway foods such as hot pies and fish and chips became established by the end of the nineteenth century.[22]

Sauces were a quick way of making cheap food palatable and tasty, both important considerations if not always appreciated at the official level. A government report produced by the Inter-Departmental Committee on Physical Deterioration in 1904 bemoaned 'desire for some sort of sensation ... dietary of pickles and vinegar'.[23] A survey the same year of some 2000 families showed that even the poorest (those with an income of less than 21s 4½d per week) on average spent more per week on meat (3s 3½d) than they did on bread (3s ½d) and had 2d to spare for condiments and pickles to enliven their meals.[24]

Figure 2. After he moved to Sheffield and changed trades to become a grocer, Henry Henderson bought a shop at 44 Green Lane. It was on the corner of the entrance to Green Lane Works. The site is now a pub beer garden. This was where Henderson was living and trading in 1885 when he mixed his first batch of relish.

Source. Photograph by the author.

It was into this world that Henderson's Relish was born, according to company legend, in 1885.[25] If that was indeed the case, then it was at 44 Green Lane that the first batch was concocted; however, the Hendersons themselves would soon be moving on. Green Lane could be a rough and ready place. The previous owner of the grocers on Green Lane, John Walster, had twice got into debt, had money and goods stolen and his wife assaulted by a neighbour.[26] It's not surprising that Henry Henderson looked elsewhere to run his business and bring up his young family. In 1889 Henderson was still listed by White's Sheffield trade directory at Green Lane, but in 1890, Kelly's directory lists him at 35 Broad Lane, closer to the commercial centre and in what must have been larger premises, judging from surviving early-twentieth century pictures of neighbouring properties.[27] He was described as a grocer despite other individuals and firms being listed as sauce manufacturers.[28] The relish was at this stage a side-line. Legend has it that it was kept in a barrel and customers had to bring their own bottles to be filled. In 1890, Henderson advertised in the *Sheffield Daily Telegraph* for a girl to fill relish bottles in the shop, signalling its growing popularity.[29]

We may reasonably wonder how Henry Henderson came up with his recipe. He would have been familiar with Yorkshire Relish and may even have sold it in his shop. Yorkshire Relish was the best-selling product of the day and the company took out advertisements to promote their product and to warn consumers about imitations. A typical example in the *Sheffield Independent* from June 1880 described Yorkshire Relish as 'The most delicious Sauce in the World', warned consumers of 'Colourable Imitations' and begged them to 'insist upon having the only genuine Yorkshire Relish'.[30] Goodall, Backhouse & Co were not afraid to go to law, spending £25,000 on legal fees between 1892 and 1900 to defend their trademarks. In 1895, they successfully took out an injunction to force the Birmingham Vinegar Co to remove their own Yorkshire Relish from sale. In court the Goodall's product was described as having a primary taste of cloves in contrast to the onion-flavour of the Birmingham version.[31]

Henderson's Relish is also flavoured with cloves, unusually for a British sauce according to Wikipedia, and like Yorkshire Relish it is a thin sauce akin to Worcestershire sauce and the earlier 'catchups'.[32] Is this a coincidence? Henry Henderson was certainly no stranger to somewhat unscrupulous business practices. In 1896, he was obliged to issue an apology in the Sheffield press after filling vinegar casks bearing the brand of Messrs Purnell, Webb & Co of Bristol with vinegar not of their manufacture.[33] He seems the kind of entrepreneur who would spot a business opportunity and not be averse to imitating what he thought was a good product. Was his own relish an attempted copy, a colourable imitation of the best seller? If so, he was wise to play down any link to Yorkshire Relish and market it under his own name.

But that may be too harsh a reading. Whether it originated in imitation or inspiration, or a bit of both, Henderson's Relish soon gained popularity and the business expanded. Through the 1890s, Henderson placed various adverts in the Sheffield papers for girls to help in the shop and for men and youths to work as porters. In 1899, he advertised for a shop assistant, giving his contact as Henry Henderson, Relish Manufacturer, indicating perhaps what he had become best known for. Most of the Sheffield trade directories continued to list him as a grocer, but in *The Sheffield City Directory* of 1900 he is listed as 'Sauce Manufacturer'.[34]

The Hendersons had three daughters, Edith, Clara Ellen and Beatrice, who may have assisted in the family business. Clara Ellen was indeed listed as a shop assistant in the 1901 census.[35] Tragedy struck in 1898, however, when Henderson's wife Clara died aged only 42. Henry remarried in 1904, a 43-year old spinster, Eliza Ann Swinnerton. The family had ceased to live above the shop by this point, having moved to Havelock Square, possibly in the aftermath of a fire in the roof at 35 Broad Lane in April 1901.[36] By 1906, the Hendersons had moved to Kenbourne Road, further out from the city centre in the salubrious and leafy suburb of Sharrow.[37] Henry decided to sell up and retire, placing an advertisement in the *Sheffield Daily Telegraph* in December 1906 advertising his grocery business making £16 weekly (a 'sure living') for sale and immediate possession.[38] The advertisements were repeated and the wording changed. In 1908, he advertised 'the business of relish manufacturer and wholesale druggist and smallware dealer to be sold', claiming it had been carried on for over half a century, double the time he had actually been trading and suggesting he may have taken over an established business either from his erstwhile partner William Eyre, or when he moved to Broad Lane. By 1909 the advertisement was changed again to read 'Illness cause leaving'.[39] The business was finally sold in 1910, nearly four years after it was first advertised for sale, possibly due to the difficulties of finding a buyer for the grocery business and the relish manufacture and possibly also because Henderson was holding out for the right price.

If he had been ill, Henry seems to have recovered and settled into a long retirement with his fortune made. He died whilst on holiday at the Granby Hotel in Skegness in 1930 and was buried next to his first wife Clara in Sheffield City Road Cemetery.[40] At his death Henry Henderson's net personal wealth was over £10000 (over £750000 in 2017 prices), but surprisingly although the notice of his death in the *Sheffield Daily Telegraph* mentions his birth in Walkeringham, his successful grocery business on Broad Lane and his membership of Nether Edge bowls club, there is nothing about his famous relish.[41]

Figure 3. Henry Henderson's grave, City Road Cemetery, Sheffield. He is buried with his first wife Clara (d.1898), his second wife Eliza (d.1933) and two of his three daughters, Edith (d.1950) and Beatrice (d.1954).

Source. Photograph by the author.

Chapter 2

Under new ownership

The Henderson family ceased to have any involvement with Henderson's Relish from 1910; however, the new owners, Shaws, jam & pickle makers from Huddersfield, retained the brand name, presumably because it had an established local following. They too were and are a family business, which is still going strong. George Shaw had variously worked as an insurance agent, a draper and a grocer across West Yorkshire before he founded the company in 1889 at Shaws Relish Works, Fitzwilliam Street, Huddersfield.[42] Evidently he had also tried his hand at relish making – Shaw's Halifax Relish was advertised in the *Halifax Courier* in 1868.[43] George Shaw was over a decade older than Henry Henderson, but was clearly convinced by the popularity of his relish and the business opportunity that it presented. He may have been prompted by his son-in-law Charles Hinksman, a former gardener and travelling salesman from Worcestershire, of all places, who had married Shaw's daughter Miriam in 1901. Hinksman was promptly installed as manager and the couple moved to Sheffield to live on Stalker Lees Road. The business was moved from the grocer's shop on Broad Lane and a small factory established at 66 Leavygreave Road, near the junction with Hounsfield Road.[44]

Figure 4. The Shaw family around the time George Shaw (seated on left) purchased Henderson's Relish.

Source. Reproduced with kind permission of Shaws (Huddersfield) Ltd.

Henderson's Relish is synonymous with Sheffield now, but in the late-nineteenth and early-twentieth centuries there were other local competitors as well as the national brands, like Yorkshire Relish. Various individuals and companies appear as sauce manufacturers in the Sheffield trade directories from the late-nineteenth and early-twentieth centuries. William Harrison of Crookes Moor Road in 1888 and Thomas Furniss of Furnival Road in 1889 are two examples. In 1906, the Coronation Sauce company, proprietor William Yeomans of Broad Street appears.[45] The name suggests the company was founded a few years earlier at the time of the coronation of Edward VII in 1901. The Coronation Sauce company continued to be listed until 1915, but then disappears from the trade directories, although its proprietor was listed as a wholesale grocer in 1916.[46]

Shaws themselves were listed in Sheffield trade directories as wholesale druggists (a general term for grocers) until 1919 when their entry changed to jam manufacturer. This reflected the parent company's trading; but, from 1923 they appeared as relish manufacturers, the business they carried on in Sheffield.[47] It was seemingly a success and growing under Shaws ownership with the experience and investment they could bring. In 1925, Shaws posted a notice in the *Sheffield Daily Telegraph* inviting tenders for one million relish bottle labels.[48] In the inter-war period, most grocers' shops were still small and independent, but increasingly they stocked branded goods sold at fixed prices.[49] The characteristic orange labels with the price printed on them in black lettering would make Henderson's Relish stand out amongst the competition on the retailers' shelves.

Company wage books from the 1920s and 1930s reveal a workforce of around a dozen people, headed by Hinksman, who was paid a salary of £5 a week. He was assisted by John Hammond and Cecil Tummon, both destined to work for the company over the next few decades.[50] Tummon was later Sales Manager, so he might have been a salesman (as Hinksman had been) involved with getting the relish bottles onto the shelves of the numerous corner shops and local grocers that supplied the folk of Sheffield with their necessaries. There was a man, or more likely a youth, doubtless to help with shifting stock and half a dozen women or girls, some of whom presumably filled the bottles (as their predecessors had done for Henderson) and one or two maybe who worked in the office. Some like the manager stayed with the company for a long time. Ada Williams, who joined just after World War One, was with the company throughout the 1920s and Rose Whitham, who joined in 1920, worked there into the 1950s, both earned around £1 12s in the 1920s. Their pay fluctuated because they were paid by the hour rather than a set weekly wage. Many others stayed for shorter periods and some were only employed in the winter when the workforce grew to 14 or 15 – Hendersons still sell more bottles in the winter than in the summer.[51]

Accounts of the costs of making 25 gallons of relish survive from the 1930s, together with the costs of packaging and a note of the percentage profit.[52] In May 1937, it cost £1 6s 2d to make 25 gallons of relish of which the biggest cost was 12s 4d for vinegar, nearly half the total. Labour was 2s for 1.5 hours. All the ingredients listed on a modern bottle of Henderson's Relish are present in the 1937 accounts except for saccharin – a more modern addition. The relish was decanted into 2 fl. oz (60 ml) and 5 fl. oz (142 ml) bottles for sale, much smaller than the 284 ml (10 fl. oz or half-pint) ones it is sold in today, although they were also producing some pint bottles, presumably for catering outlets. Bottling and packing was manually intensive: filling the bottles by hand, pasting on the labels, sealing with a cork and wax and then packing with brown paper and string. Producing a gross (144) of 2 fl. oz bottles cost 6s 2½d with the relish itself costing just under 2s. A gross of 5 fl. oz bottles cost 11s 3½d with the cost of the relish being 4s 9½d. Bottles and packaging were over half the cost for the 5 fl. oz bottles and two-thirds for the 2 fl. oz bottles. A marginal note reveals profits were around 25 per cent.

The company wage books and the notes on the cost and profits of making relish from 1937 permit some interesting calculations. In March 1938, the weekly wage bill for 14 employees came to £25 18s. Assuming similar wages were paid throughout the year the annual wage bill would have been over £1300. With profits around 4s on a gross of 5 fl. oz bottles, Shaws would need to have sold over 900000 5 fl. oz bottles of relish just to meet the wages bill alone – 1.8 million of the 2 fl. oz bottles. The population of Sheffield in 1931 was 562822, similar to what it had been in 1921 and would remain about the same until a slight decline in the late-twentieth century.[53] Given that most sales would have been within the city, the average household must have got through several bottles of relish a year, maybe a dozen or more for some. It's clear that by the 1930s and probably a decade earlier given the notice in the *Sheffield Daily Telegraph* for a million labels, Hendo's was becoming established as Sheffield's favourite sauce.

Figure 5. The site of the first Henderson's Relish factory established in 1910 by Shaws at 66 Leavygreave Road. Little remains of the original building apart from the doorway to the right of the graffiti-covered wall.

Source. Photograph by the author.

Chapter 3

A new company

As the spectre of another war loomed over Europe, changes were happening at the relish factory. In summer 1939, Miriam Hinksman died aged 70. By early 1940, Charles Hinksman had married Gladys Freeman, a 48-year old journalist, 15 years his junior. The change in his personal circumstances seems to have prompted Charles into a momentous decision: he bought the relish factory from Shaws and formed an independent company, Hendersons Relish Limited. For their part Shaws may have been happy to sell. The relish factory in Sheffield had remained an outlier to their main business producing pickles and jams at their factory in Huddersfield. Nevertheless, the Shaw family had a seat on the board and shares in the new company.

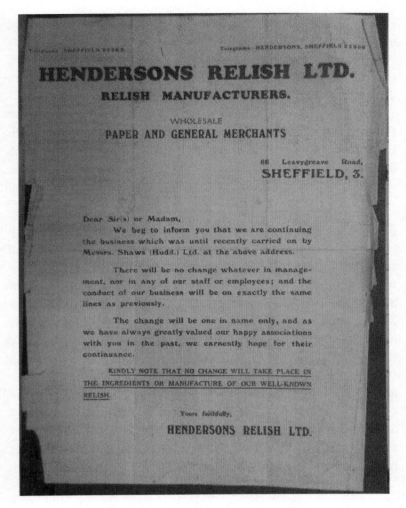

Figure 6. Hendersons Relish Limited issued a flyer to inform their customers that there would be no change in the management, staff and crucially in the ingredients or manufacture of 'our well-known relish' (in capitals and underlined for emphasis).

Source. Reproduced by kind permission of Hendersons (Sheffield) Limited.

Hendersons Relish Limited held its inaugural meeting on 12 January 1940 at the offices of Messrs Pontefract & Porritt, Chartered Accountants on Railway Street, Huddersfield. Hinksman was installed as chairman of the directors, company secretary and managing director. Cecil Tummon was also made a director and sales manager. Robert Howard of Leeds and Norman Shaw of Huddersfield, Hinksman's nephew and head of Shaws, were the other two directors. Capital was raised by issuing 4648 shares at £1 each, Hinksman holding a majority of these.[54]

The finances of the new company sorted, a handbill was issued (see Figure 6) to reassure customers that the change was in name only; the management, the staff and crucially the relish would stay the same.[55] Hinksman clearly knew what he was doing having run the company for 30 years. At the first annual general meeting in 1941, a 10 per cent dividend was announced for shareholders, Tummon received a £100 bonus and Hinksman saw his salary increased to £520, effectively double what he had been earning as manager of the relish factory under Shaws ownership a few years previously. In the euphoria Charles even got the shareholders to agree to the company buying his 20hp Rover for £100, because it was used 'exclusively' on company business. Cecil Tummon bought another 225 shares and Mr Porritt, the accountant, showed his faith in the new venture by buying 100 shares himself.[56]

Running a business in wartime brought challenges, however. An early task was to seek space outside Sheffield in case 66 Leavygreave Road was destroyed in an enemy air-raid. Hinksman and Tummon secured rent on a room in Stoney Middleton, Derbyshire at 4s per week. Profits suffered in 1943 due to the difficulties of securing raw materials and labour, but the company continued to pay dividends to its shareholders and bonuses to the directors.[57]

Figure 7. Charles Hinksman in later life. A native of Worcestershire, Hinksman married Miriam Shaw and was installed as the manager of the relish factory under Shaws ownership. His wife died in 1939 and within the year he had bought the relish factory from Shaws and set up his own company, Hendersons Relish Limited. He married Gladys Freeman shortly after.

Source. Photograph reproduced by kind permission of Hendersons (Sheffield) Limited.

In the post war years production was mechanised. In November 1948, Hinksman took a trip to London to view a new vacuum filling machine for bottling relish and agreed to purchase it and an electric motor for £100. In January 1950, the company purchased a 'Newman' precision bottle labelling machine, again with electric motor, for £250.[58] There was to be no more manually filling bottles and fiddling with corks and wax seals. The number of employees remained at around a dozen and presumably production increased due to mechanisation.[59] Profits certainly rose, topping £4000 in 1950 and over £5000 in 1952.[60]

Notes from 1953 show that that it now cost £4 2s 6d to make 25 gallons of relish, with vinegar still the single largest cost at £1 16s 9d for 18.75 gallons – Hendo's was 75 per cent vinegar at this date. The relish was now being sold in larger 6 fl. oz and 10 fl. oz bottles with screw caps. Producing a gross of 6 fl. oz bottles in February 1953 cost £2 3s 4½d and the same of 10 fl. oz bottles £3 3s 4d. The calculations for labour suggest that mechanisation hadn't necessarily brought savings on that front, but the product packaging had been kept up to date. Profits were calculated at just over 30 per cent wholesale and just under 40 per cent retail, with two-thirds of sales being wholesale.[61] On that assumption the average profit on a gross of 6 fl. oz bottles would have been £1 2s 7d. The staff wage bill in August 1951 was £61 13s 5d for 11 people and again assuming similar wages for the whole year would have given an annual wage bill of over £3000. To meet these costs and achieve profits of £5000 as they did in the early 1950s, Hendersons must have been selling over 1 million 6 fl. oz bottles per year, enough relish for every man, woman and child in Sheffield to have over half a pint each.

The new packaging and mechanisation were important, because Hendersons needed to move with the times and maintain their market share against other brands. Kelly's trade directory from 1933 reveals another local competitor: Mrs Florence Todd's Victor Brand of sauces. In the late 1940s and into the 1950s, Mrs Todd took out adverts in the Sheffield trade directories. This was something Hendersons had never done. Hinksman and Tummon may have looked askance at such methods as a waste of money. They may have been right at the time, because the Victor brand disappeared from the Sheffield trade directories by 1957 and from that date on Hendersons were the only sauce manufacturers listed.[62] Sheffield was becoming a one sauce town.

In December 1951, Charles Hinksman, by now 75, handed over the role of managing director to his old partner, Cecil Tummon. Charles died a little over a year later in May 1953. He had managed the company for over 40 years, taking it from a side-line run from a grocer's shop to an independent and very profitable business. Hinksman's role as chairman of directors and secretary was taken by his widow, Gladys. Her first move was to appoint her 50-year old brother, Neville Freeman, to the board of directors. Poor Cecil Tummon, combining the roles of managing director and Sales Manager died in March 1954. He was only 54. Neville took over as managing director soon after. Brother and sister were to run the company for the next 30 years. Neville owned the Faircut Tool company in Sheffield and seemingly continuing a trend his company Ford Consul Mk1 was sold to Hendersons for £650.[63]

The 1950s were boom years for Hendersons. Profits continued to rise, hitting a high of £5303 6s 10d in 1956.[64] Pauline Climpson, publisher of the first Henderson's Relish cookbook in 1998, who grew up in Sheffield at this time, described every fish and chip shop and pie and pea shop having a bottle of Henderson's Relish on the counter.[65] These takeaway food outlets were popular with ordinary Sheffielders and helped cement Hendo's relationship with the city. It was the time when Harold Macmillan told the British public that they had 'never had it so good' and in Sheffield the relish was doubtless being lashed more liberally than before. At the relish factory, staff benefitted as wages were increased to retain workers in an age of full employment. In April 1954, workers formerly paid by time (Ada Arrows, Mary Steel and Dorothy

Thompson) were put on the regular staff pay roll. Neville Freeman reviewed the wages of several experienced hands in the light of Board of Trade instructions in November 1954 and revised them upwards again in January 1955. Mrs Jean Bell, an experienced shop-hand, saw her wages rise initially from £4 3s 6d per week to £4 13s and then to £5.[66]

As the decade drew to a close, however, a cloud appeared on the horizon. Many small corner shops were being swept away as part of town planning. These had been the traditional retail outlets for Henderson's Relish for a generation or more and the company was going to have to deal with a different type of retailer, supermarkets that might not appreciate a brand with strictly local appeal. Concerns were expressed at the annual general meeting in 1958 about the marketing methods of the 'multiples' as they were termed and the rise in staff wages. The response was surprising. In August, Gladys recommended to a meeting of directors that the company change its name to remove the word 'Relish', because it formed a 'considerably smaller portion' of the company's turnover. The name was officially changed to Hendersons (Sheffield) Limited on 1 December 1958.[67] The new company name was approved on condition of their not being involved in the cutlery trade and continuing to be based in Sheffield. It seems a strange decision today and it's not clear what else formed part of the company's turnover at the time, but maybe Gladys and Neville saw a future in which relish manufacture might not be what Hendersons was primarily known for.[68]

The following year the company was forced to move from 66 Leavygreave Road due to the expansion of the University, but Neville secured a new site further down the same road at 41, which was to be the home of Hendersons for the next 50 years. The acquisition of the new premises, however, cost £3158 6s 6d.[69] Into the 1960s annual profits declined, frequently dipping below £3000 (in real terms less than half what they had been in the 1950s). The continued closure of small shops and the difficulty of dealing with 'large combines and multiple concerns whose business methods were rigid and anonymous' was mentioned at the annual general meeting in 1964 and became a regular refrain at subsequent meetings. There were also particular issues with a spate of sickness in 1964 that had affected the company's small workforce and bad debts owed to Hendersons by Sheffield Wholesale Grocers in 1967 and 1968.[70]

Nevertheless, with the canny brother and sister duo at the helm, Hendersons was able to weather the storm. In 1966, notes and calculations on the cost of producing relish were made once more. Producing 25 gallons of relish cost £4 12s 6d, not much more than it had over a decade earlier; however, vinegar, the main constituent and cost, was now diluted with half as much water – the vinegar content of Hendo's being reduced from 75 to 50 per cent. Producing a gross of 6 fl. oz bottles cost £3 1s 8d and the same amount of 10 fl. oz bottles cost £4 5s 3d, similar to what they had done in the early 1950s; but, in line with inflation retail and wholesale prices were more than double. Hendersons were now making over 100 per cent profit on retail sales and over 80 per cent on wholesale.[71]

At the first annual general meeting of the new decade in November 1970, Neville Freeman stated, 'that in time not so very far ahead he thought it would be a better paying proposition to handle Relish only'. This suggests that whatever direction they thought the company might take a decade or so earlier, the focus now was firmly on relish. Freeman also said that Hendersons were 'learning to do without the small shops'.[72] In fact, a directors meeting in 1958 mentioned a payment of 1.25 per cent of sales to Mr Stoakley for new Co-Op accounts, suggesting he had brokered a deal for Hendersons with the Co-Op – E.O. Stoakley appears in the wages books and left the company in October 1978.[73] The company could not escape the general economic slump of the 1970s, however. Dividends fell, reaching a low of 3.33 per cent in 1977, which must have challenged Neville's earlier sanguine outlook.[74] In the face of falling dividends, and arguably benefitting from them, Neville sought to consolidate his holding on Hendersons shares, buying out many of the original shareholders or their descendants. By the end of the decade, he was the second largest shareholder after his sister and between them they owned over two-thirds of the company stock.[75]

Figure 8. The Henderson's Relish factory at 41 Leavygreave Road, Sheffield. This site was the home of Henderson's Relish from 1959 to 2013. The expansion of the University of Sheffield had forced Hendersons to move once before and was a continued threat in the 1990s and 2000s.

Source. Photograph by the author.

A visit to the factory in 1981 by the *Sheffield Star* newspaper provided the first pictures of the interior of the factory and probably the first that most people in Sheffield had seen.[76] In the accompanying article, Neville, then aged 79, quipped to the reporter, 'You've not come to anywhere very exciting, you know'. But Hendo's was now a legend. Sheffield's own Charlie and the Chocolate Factory – was it run by a mysterious band of Yorkshire oompah-loompahs? The *Star* was about to reveal all. Their pictures show what amounted to quite literally a cottage industry. An ageing workforce, operating ageing machinery in a two-storey Victorian house and its outbuildings. The endearing charm of these images no doubt spoke to local pride in Hendo's, their relish, but they also illustrate why the product was unknown outside the city and its immediate environs. Production capacity was limited: 7000 bottles per week in summer up to 10000 in winter. 'If you mention Henderson's Relish in Rotherham, they don't know what you're talking about', said Neville. Staff numbers were down to six or seven, around half what they had been in the 1950s. 'We've had fewer and fewer staff and get more and more done ... We don't reckon to be up to date', added Neville, also revealing that he never used the relish himself.[77]

Neville's reticence disguised the fact that he and his sister had done well out of Hendersons over the three decades they had been running the company. On the other hand, Hendersons had benefitted in that it had remained in existence as an independent company. Henry Henderson after all had sold up at the age of 60 and retired on the proceeds. Gladys and Neville could have done the same. In fact, Gladys did retire soon afterward in 1982, at the age of 90, phoning her brother to resign as chairman of the board and transferring her shares to him. Neville appointed accountant Mr J.G. Richmond as director. Richmond was an accountant with Messrs Wells, Richardson & Co. who had taken over Hendersons accounts in

1974. At a board meeting in December 1984, it was agreed that Richmond was to deal with general finance matters in future to relieve some of the pressure on Neville. It sounded like one chapter was closing and another was about to begin. Indeed, it was, Neville died early in 1985.[78]

Chapter 4

The Modern Way

At the board meeting following Neville's death in March 1985, his widow Connie was appointed as a director. Mrs L. Richmond was also appointed to the board as secretary. In September of the same year, Mr Richmond became acting chairman. At the next meeting in December, Richmond outlined a number of sensible packaging changes: introducing pourers to the bottles and removing the price from the labels (in 1981 Neville had shown the *Sheffield Star* reporter stacks of old unused labels at various prices and acknowledged that the bottles would not pour without spilling). Continuing, he described the factory machinery as old. There was trouble with the vacuum bottle filler (the one purchased in 1948) and they could really do with replacing the entire production line. Richmond also revealed there was a lot of machinery from Neville's Faircut Tool Company on the premises at Leavygreave Road. He was going to look at disposing of this to Kelham Island Museum.[79]

Undoubtedly correct in his analysis of the business, Richmond may not have endeared himself to Connie, who crucially was the majority shareholder. Something happened. The minutes don't give the reason why, but on 30 September 1986 it was recorded that both Richmond and his wife had resigned a week or so previously. The same minutes also recorded the appointment of Connie's nephew, Dr Kenneth Freeman, as director and secretary. A month later, Kenneth Freeman attended his first annual general meeting as a director of Hendersons. Also present was Malcolm Tummon (Cecil's son), Connie Freeman and the auditor J.A. Hunt. Rumours of a takeover were voiced and those attending were put on their guard to protect the interests of shareholders (chiefly their own interests).[80]

In 1987, Gladys died at the grand age of 96. A generation was passing. In 1991, Kenneth Freeman took over from his aunt Connie as managing director and chairman. His wife Pamela became secretary. After the boom years of the 1950s, Hendersons had atrophied in the 1970s and 1980s. Richmond had highlighted some changes, but there were two major issues that needed addressing if the business was to have any future in the modern world: accommodation and marketing.

The spectre of another compulsory purchase order on their premises had been raised as early as 1982. At that time Martin Shaw, joint owner of Shaws, offered space at their factory in Huddersfield. In 1989, with eight years remaining on the current lease and structural defects in the premises, the board decided to look at alternatives. In 1990, it was again suggested to move production to Shaws in Huddersfield.[81] Shaws had long-standing links with Hendersons and in fact supplied them with vinegar into the 1990s;[82] however, one wonders whether Hendersons of Huddersfield would have survived, so entwined is the relish with its home city. In the end, a move out of Sheffield wasn't required and the lease was renewed, but the issue rumbled on through the 1990s and into the 2000s. An article in the *Sheffield Telegraph* in August 2001 stated that the firm was 'being forced to leave its traditional home in Leavygreave Road due to redevelopment'.[83] That proved to be premature and the redevelopment was postponed. The cost of new premises was a concern, but the opportunity to expand production and gain SALSA (Safe and Local Supplier Approval) accreditation to secure supermarket sales eventually drove the decision and Hendersons moved to their new factory off the Parkway in November 2013.[84]

Figure 9. Hendersons (Sheffield) Limited new factory off Sheffield Parkway. The company moved here in 2013.

Source. Photograph by the author.

Like his uncle, Kenneth Freeman realised the company faced challenges in a retail market increasingly dominated by supermarkets, but he needed to resolve it quickly. The first moves were to raise the profile of Henderson's Relish. When Sheffield's two football clubs, United and Wednesday got to the FA Cup Semi-Final in 1993, Hendersons produced commemorative bottles in the team colours. They were a hit and continue to be produced, allowing football fans to show their love for their favourite club and their favourite sauce at the same time.

More was needed, though. In an interview with the *Sheffield Telegraph* in 1995, manager, Kath Spivey, was keen to scotch rumours of closure; however, there were just three other employees and production was down to 2400 bottles per week, most sold within 25 miles of Sheffield.[85] Up to the 1990s, Hendersons had only ever dealt with one supermarket chain, the Co-Op. In 1996, Kenneth Freeman signed a deal to retail Henderson's Relish through Sainsburys.[86] Simon Webster was appointed as marketing manager to set about getting Henderson's Relish noticed. Their efforts bore fruit. In March 1998, the *Sheffield Star* reported production was up to around 500000 bottles a year, higher than when they visited back in 1981 and with only four staff. Most was still sold locally, but discount supermarket Netto were now also stocking it.[87] The following year Hendersons set up a website with the help of some local web designers. Global interest and sales were envisaged. After the first day online, the company received an astonishing 34 emails, mainly from ex-pat Sheffielders enquiring where they could get supplies of Hendo's.[88] This was the early days of the internet.

By the 1990s tastes were changing. Pie and mash and fish and chips were competing with Italian, Chinese and Indian foods in an increasingly diverse city. Henderson's Relish needed to appeal to a more diverse audience and one that was used to a greater range of foods. At the same time, there was also a growing interest in the best of traditional British food. In 1998, Hendersons organised a competition amongst local chefs to produce dishes, both modern and traditional, incorporating Hendo's. The best entries were published in a cookbook, with anecdotes from celebrity 'Relish Rooters' the aim being to 'raise awareness of using Relish as a cooking ingredient'.[89] A second cookbook was published in 2014, lavishly illustrated with artwork from Peter McKee and host of other local artists for whom Hendo's was a source (or sauce) of inspiration. A new gallery of celebrities contributed recipes, revealing Hendo's as the store cupboard solution to enliven the modern British culinary repertoire across the political spectrum, from David Blunkett's Shepherd's Pie to Nick Clegg's pasta bake. Ironically, we also find this relish made of exotic eastern ingredients being used by long-established Sheffield Indian restaurant, Ashoka, in their house puris.[90]

Figure 10. Dr Kenneth Freeman. Dr Freeman reinvigorated the company's fortunes after he took over as managing director in 1991.

Source. Reproduced by kind permission of Hendersons (Sheffield) Ltd.

Kenneth Freeman died in December 2013, having brought Hendersons through a potentially difficult period, which could have seen production leave Sheffield and maybe finish for good. The company now appears to be stronger than ever. Testament to the work Kenneth and his staff put in and that is being carried on by his widow, Pamela, their children, who are both directors and the current team, headed by general manager, Matt Davies. In the new factory production has expanded and with it the capability, to reach a bigger market.[91] Further investment has been made in automation for the production line, including a new bottle filling machine, capping machine and self-adhesive labeller (a far cry from the corks, wax seals and gum used to paste on the labels back in the 1930s). In December 2019, a third Henderson's Relish cookbook was published, written by Katie Fisher (author of numerous regional cookery collections) with cover art by another local artist, Matt Brewin.[92] Its title is 'Strong and Northern', a phrase that Hendersons have started using recently, emphasising the northern heritage of the product. The last survivor of the sauces and relishes produced in Sheffield and other northern towns and cities over the previous century and a half. But, of course, Hendo's distant origins in part at least lie in the 'catchups' first encountered in the Far East by British merchants in the seventeenth century, so it seems appropriate that in 2021 Hendersons are due to start exporting relish to Japan.

And what of Yorkshire Relish? Its history offers a sobering tale. Poor leadership and death duties hampered Goodall, Backhouse & Co and in 1959 it was sold to Hammonds, a regional player rather than a national one. Hammonds themselves were bought by Pillsbury in 1982. Three years later, the flagship Leeds factory was closed and production moved to Bradford. In 1991, Hammonds was acquired by Albert Fisher Group. Yorkshire Relish was at this time available in thin, thick, spicy and fruity varieties. In 1996, a relaunch of Yorkshire Relish (in thick variety only) failed to ignite sales to the levels demanded by the corporate owners and the brand was discontinued in 2001.[93] An ignominious end to what had once been the best-selling sauce in the country.

So, what is the secret of the success of Henderson's Relish? Undoubtedly, taste has a lot to do with it. Henry Henderson clearly hit on a good recipe. Down the years it has been tweaked with the proportion of vinegar being reduced and saccharin added, shifting the balance between sour and sweet, arguably following wider changes in taste. The spices and flavourings have remained the same, however, and the familiarity of the taste, redolent of home, is key to Hendo's appeal to its traditional fans – working-class Sheffielders. This is a paradox considering that Hendo's is made from exotic and perhaps unfamiliar ingredients (in 1981 the *Sheffield Star* had to explain to their readers what a tamarind was), but the creation and use of such relishes and sauces has a long history in British cuisine and those flavours have forged an identity.

Hendo's has also attracted new followers, in part through marketing, but also through people moving to Sheffield and encountering the relish. Expansion of the university, which could have forced Hendersons out of the city at one stage, has ended up contributing to its resurgence by providing a host of potential new customers, many of them new to cooking. Henderson's Relish here benefits from being both a condiment to add to food at the table and an ingredient in cooking. This versatility distinguishes Hendo's from a lot of its competitors and was also a selling point for the original thin Yorkshire Relish. Goodall, Backhouse & Co produced books of recipes incorporating their relish back in its late-nineteenth and early-twentieth century heyday. It also helps in an age when many consumers are increasingly concerned about what ingredients are in their food that Henderson's Relish is vegan, gluten-free and relatively low in salt.

And taste in another sense is important, too. Hendersons have made the most in the last 20 years of celebrity endorsements and associations. Both of Sheffield's football teams and local sports star and Olympic champion, Jessica Ennis-Hill have had labels celebrating their achievements. The pop stars and the artists of the steel city have lent their aid to the cause. It's cool to like Hendo's. Both Richard Hawley and the Arctic Monkeys have commissioned special edition labels for their album releases. This of course plays well to an audience of students.

But taste isn't the whole story. The history of the business is important. The long period of management by Charles Hinksman was crucial, developing the product commercially under Shaws ownership and then setting up an independent company and latterly introducing mechanisation to the production line. Similarly, Kenneth Freeman's period of tenure brought the company out of the doldrums and set it on course for navigating the modern retail world with the importance of marketing, the internet and supermarkets. Even the period under Neville Freeman and his sister, Gladys, was significant, because although commercial growth might have been limited, particularly from the 1960s to the 1980s, the very fact that production and distribution didn't expand beyond the city limits meant that Hendo's engrained itself in Sheffielders' sense of identity; it was something peculiar to them.

The new identity being forged for Henderson's Relish, however, is wider than just Sheffield. 'Strong and Northern' is the phrase on the latest cookbook and on the T-shirts that can be purchased from their online store. Henderson's Relish represents the north of England, not just Sheffield. As an interesting coda, a recent label had a Yorkshire Rose and proclaimed Hendo's as 'The Yorkshire Original'. The local Yorkshire Crisps company (based near Sheffield) has a Yorkshire Sauce flavour, flavoured with Henderson's Relish. It seems that finally, and without a legal shot being fired, Hendersons have taken on the Yorkshire Relish mantle. It's to be hoped they don't end up going the same way and that we can continue to enjoy the great taste of Hendo's for many years to come.

A Saucy Tale. The History of Henderson's Relish

Endnotes

¹ *Recipes to Relish* (Sheffield, 1998), pp. 19-21.
² https://www.theguardian.com/music/2013/oct/27/arctic-monkeys-mexico-beatlemania, accessed 27/02/2020.
³ P. Freeman and J. Food, *The Henderson's Relish Cookbook* (Sheffield, 2014), p. 28.
⁴ Freeman and Food, *The Henderson's Relish Cookbook*, p. 144.
⁵ *Tom Wrigglesworth's Hang-Ups*, 2016. Episode 2, Big Tom and the Hendersons. BBC Radio 4. 09/09/2016.
⁶ This artwork was used as the cover on Freeman and Food, *The Henderson's Relish Cookbook*.
⁷ 'Henry Henderson' (1851), *Census return for Walkeringham, Nottinghamshire, Owston sub-district*. Public Record Office: PRO HO107/2119, folio 428, p. 26; 'Henry Henderson' (1861), *Census return for Walkeringham, Nottinghamshire, Misteron sub-district*. Public Record Office: PRO RG9/2407, folio 64, p. 4. Available at https://ancestry.co.uk, accessed 11/04/2020.
⁸ When he died in February 1902, Joseph Henderson, senior had real estate valued at over £4000. The farm was advertised for sale and described as 63 acres of grass and arable in a high state of cultivation, having been farmed by the owner for over 70 years. *Sheffield Daily Telepgraph*, 8/2/1902 and 13/2/1902. Joseph Henderson, senior had sold one parcel of over 8 acres of pasture in 1880. *Sheffield Daily Telegraph*, 16/9/1880.
⁹ *Sheffield Daily Telegraph*, 20/5/1920. Joseph was an avid reader of the *Telegraph* and an article celebrated his golden wedding as well as giving a brief history of his life and the fact that his father had been born and lived for over 90 years on their farm in Walkeringham. He seems to have remained close to his brother.

10 'Henry Henderson' (1871), *Census return for Haxey, Lincolnshire, Owston sub-district*. Public Record Office: PRO RG10/3440, folio 9, p. 11. Available at https://ancestry.co.uk, accessed 11/04/2020.
11 Information about Burnham or Brock's Mill from https://historicengland.org.uk/listing/the-list/list-entry/1346725, accessed 14/03/2020.
12 https://www.freebmd.org.uk/cgi/information.pl?cite=hY3IUcctOmA3%2BTmvJzAomQ&scan=1, accessed 14/03/2020.
13 'Henry Henderson' (1881), *Census return for Furnival St No. 2 Ct. 5, Sheffield, Yorkshire, South Sheffield sub-district*. Public Record Office: PRO 4650, folio 58, p. 30. Available at https://ancestry.co.uk, accessed 11/04/2020.
14 *Sheffield Independent*, 23/09/1882.
15 J. Burnett, *Plenty and Want. A Social History of Food in England from 1815 to the Present Day* (2013), p. 121.
16 Kelly's Directories Ltd., *Directory of Sheffield and Rotherham 1883* (London, 1883).
17 G. Lehmann, *The British Housewife. Cookery Books, Cooking and Society in Eighteenth-Century Britain* (Totnes, 2003), pp. 47, 248-9.
18 A. Davidson, *The Oxford Companion to Food* (Oxford, 1999), p. 430; L. Mason and C. Brown, *Traditional Foods of Britain. An Inventory* (Totnes, 1999), p. 324.
19 P. Atkins, 'Vinegar and Sugar; the early history of factory-made jams, pickles and sauces in Britain', in D.J. Oddy and A. Drouard (eds), *The Food Industries of Europe in the Nineteenth and Twentieth Centuries* (Farnham, 2013), p. 42.
20 Atkins, 'Vinegar and Sugar', pp. 43, 51.
21 http://letslookagain.com/2015/02/goodall-backhouse-co-yorkshire-relish/, accessed 22/05/2018; Mason and Brown (eds), *Traditional Foods of Britain*, pp. 330-1.
22 Burnett, *Plenty and Want*, pp. 117-8, 165.
23 D.J. Oddy, 'Working-Class diets in Late Nineteenth-Century Britain', *Economic History Review* 2nd Series, Volume 23 (1970), 322.
24 Burnett, *Plenty and Want*, p. 185.
25 Freeman and Food, *The Henderson's Relish Cookbook*, p. 10.
26 *Sheffield Independent*, 16/8/1876; *Sheffield Independent*, 01/07/1880; *Sheffield Daily Telegraph*, 15/7/1880.

[27] Kelly's Directories Ltd., *White's General Commercial Directory of Sheffield and Rotherham 1889* (London, 1889); Kelly's Directories Ltd., *Directory of Sheffield and Rotherham 1890* (London, 1890); https://picturesheffeld.com has early twentieth century pictures of properties on Broad Lane, but alas none of number 35.

[28] Kelly's Directories Ltd., *Directory of Sheffield and Rotherham 1890* (London, 1890).

[29] Freeman and Food, *The Henderson's Relish Cookbook*, p. 14; *Sheffield Daily Telegraph*, 08/02/1890.

[30] *Sheffield Independent*, 15/6/1880.

[31] http://letslookagain.com/2015/02/goodall-backhouse-co-yorkshire-relish/, accessed 22/05/2018; the result of the case against the Birmingham Vinegar Company was reported in *Sheffield Independent*, 30/10/1895.

[32] https://en.wikipedia.org/wiki/Henderson%27s_Relish, accessed 21/03/2020.

[33] *Sheffield Daily Telegraph*, 16/10/1896.

[34] *Sheffield Daily Telegraph*, 19/08/1893; *Sheffield Daily Telegraph*, 06/06/1896; Henderson is listed as a relish manufacturer in an advert placed in *Sheffield Daily Telegraph*, 27/07/1899; Pawson & Brailsford, *The Sheffield City Directory 1900* (Sheffield, 1900).

[35] 'Henry Henderson' (1901), *Census return for 67 Havelock Square, Sheffield, Yorkshire, Ecclesall Bierlow sub-district.* Public Record Office: PRO 4350, folio 73, p. 16. Available at https://ancestry.co.uk, accessed 11/04/2020.

[36] *Sheffield Daily Telegraph*, 27/4/1901.

[37] Pawson & Brailsford, *The Sheffield City Directory 1900*; W. White, *General Directory and Commercial Directory of Sheffield 1906* (London, 1906).

[38] *Sheffield Daily Telegraph*, 05/12/1906.

[39] *Sheffield Daily Telegraph*, 05/12/1908.

[40] His second wife and his two spinster daughters, Beatrice and Edith, would later also be buried in the same plot. Henderson's middle daughter, Clara Ellen, married Frederick Fox and died in 1969.

[41] *Leeds Mercury*, 20/11/1930; *Sheffield Daily Telegraph*, 8/9/1930.

[42] https://shaws1889.com/our-story/, accessed 11/01/2019.

[43] *Halifax Courier*, 26/12/1868.

---

[44] https://picturesheffeld.com, y01263 is a photograph taken in 1948 of the corner of Leavygreave Road and Hounsfield Road with the old Henderson's factory visible on the right hand side.

[45] Kelly's Directories Ltd., *Directory of Sheffield and Rotherham 1888* (London, 1888); W. White, *General Directory and Commercial Directory of Sheffield 1889* (London, 1889); White, *General Directory and Commercial Directory of Sheffield 1906.*

[46] W. White, *General Directory and Commercial Directory of Sheffield 1915* (London, 1915); W. White, *General Directory and Commercial Directory of Sheffield 1916* (London, 1916).

[47] W. White, *General Directory and Commercial Directory of Sheffield 1919* (London, 1919); Kelly's Directories Ltd., *Directory of Sheffield and Rotherham 1923* (London, 1923).

[48] *Sheffield Daily Telegraph*, 06/07/1925.

[49] Burnett, *Plenty and Want*, p. 260.

[50] The company wages books, minute books and notebook are held by Hendersons (Sheffield) Ltd. They are uncatalogued and were viewed with kind permission of Matt Davies, general manager. The wages books run from the time of Shaws ownership to the early 1980s. Individual books cover one or more years and are of varying sizes and formats.

[51] Hendersons Wages Books; Matt Davies, personal communication.

[52] Notebook held by Hendersons (Sheffield) Ltd. This is a slim volume with ruled and lined pages that are un-numbered. It was evidently used for periodically recording the costs of producing 25 gallons of relish and the subsequent costs for bottling and packaging.

[53] *Sheffield's Population Statistics 1086-2001*, Sheffield City Council (2015).

[54] Hendersons Minute Books, Volume 1. The first volume of minutes runs from the formation of the company in 1940 to 1971. The initial pages are un-numbered.

[55] A copy of the handbill was pasted into Volume 1 of the Hendersons Minute Books.

[56] Hendersons Minute Books, Volume 1, pp. 10-12.

[57] Hendersons Minute Books, Volume 1, pp. 14-18.

[58] Hendersons Minute Books, Volume 1, pp. 41, 45.

[59] Hendersons Wages Books.

[60] Hendersons Minute Books, Volume 1, pp. 47-56.

[61] Hendersons Notebook.

[62] Kelly's Directories Ltd., *Directory of Sheffield and Rotherham 1933* (London,1933). The volumes for 1948, 1951, 1957 were also consulted.

[63] Hendersons Minute Books, Volume 1, pp. 54, 59-60, 67, 69, 80.

[64] Hendersons Minute Books, Volume 1, p. 81.

[65] *Recipes to Relish*, p. 6.

[66] Hendersons Minute Books, Volume 1, pp. 69, 74-5.

[67] Hendersons Minute Books, Volume 1, pp. 86-8.

[68] The handbill issued in 1940 (see figure 5) described the company as wholesale paper and general merchants, but it's not clear what contribution this made to the company turnover.

[69] Hendersons Minute Books, Volume 1, p. 157.

[70] Hendersons Minute Books, Volume 1, pp. 101, 112, 115, 118, 169.

[71] Hendersons Notebook.

[72] Hendersons Minute Books, Volume 1, un-numbered.

[73] Hendersons Minute Books, Volume 1, un-numbered; Hendersons Wages Books.

[74] Hendersons Minute Books, Volume 2, p. 2.

[75] Hendersons Minute Books, Volume 1, pp. 63, 87, un-numbered; Hendersons Minute Books, Volume 2, pp. 3, 5.

[76] The photographs from the Sheffield Star's visits in 1981 and 1987 can be seen on https://picturesheffield.com, images S28297, s28298 and s28299.

[77] *Sheffield Star*, 08/09/1981.

[78] Hendersons Minute Books, Volume 2, pp. 11-16, 21.

[79] Hendersons Minute Books, Volume 2, pp. 22-6.

[80] Hendersons Minute Books, Volume 2, pp. 33, 157.

[81] Hendersons Minute Books, Volume 2, pp. 16, 161-2.

[82] Information supplied by Matthew Shaw, chairman of Shaws, via email 10/11/2020.

[83] *Sheffield Telegraph*, 24/08/2001.

[84] Freeman and Food, *The Henderson's Relish Cookbook*, p. 34.

[85] *Sheffield Telegraph*, 07/07/1995, p. 13.

[86] Freeman and Food, *The Henderson's Relish Cookbook*, p. 22.

[87] *Sheffield Star*, 14/03/1998.

[88] *Sheffield Gazette*, 25/11/1999.

89 *Recipes to Relish, p. 7.*
90 Freeman and Food, *The Henderson's Relish Cookbook.*
91 https://www.yorkshirepost.co.uk/business/profile-on-matt-davies-new-boss-relishes-challenge-of-growing-henderson-s-sales-1-8433079, accessed 12/03/2020.
92 K. Fisher, *Strong and Northern* (2019).
93 http://letslookagain.com/2015/02/goodall-backhouse-co-yorkshire-relish/, accessed 22/05/2018.

Timeline

1850	Henry Henderson is born.
1885	Henry Henderson makes his first batch of Henderson's Relish.
1910	Henry Henderson sells his business to Shaws. Charles Hinksman is installed as manager. Production is moved to a factory at 66 Leavygreave Road.
1940	Charles Hinksman buys the business from Shaws. Hendersons Relish Ltd is founded.
1953	Gladys Hinksman invites her brother Neville Freeman to be a director.
1954	Neville Freeman becomes managing director.
1958	The company name is changed to Hendersons (Sheffield) Ltd.
1959	The relish factory is moved to 41 Leavygreave Road.
1991	Dr Kenneth Freeman becomes managing director.
2013	Production is moved to a new factory on Sheffield Parkway.

Index

Arctic Monkeys, The, 1, 36
Arrows, Ada, 23
Bean, Sean, 1
Bell, Jean, 24
Birmingham Vinegar Company, 9
Blunkett, David (former MP for Sheffield Brightside), 33
Brewin, Matt, 34
Broad Lane, Sheffield, 9-11, 13
Brock, Robert (miller of Low Burnham), 3
catchup, 6, 9, 34
Clegg, Nick (former MP for Sheffield Hallam), 33
Climpson, Pauline, 23
Cock's Reading Sauce, 6
Coronation Sauce Company, Sheffield, 14
Davies, Matt, vi, ix, 34
Def Leppard, 1
Doncaster, South Yorkshire, 3
Dowd, Jim (MP for Lewisham), 2
Earl Street, Sheffield, 5
Ennis-Hill, Jessica, 36
Eyre, William, 5, 11
Faircut Tools Company, 23, 29
Freeman, Connie, 29-30
Freeman, Kenneth, 30-32, *33*, 34, 36
Freeman, Neville, x, 23-9, 36
Freeman, Pamela, vi, 30, 34
Furniss, Thomas (sauce manufacturer), 14

Furnival Street, Sheffield, 4
Goodall, Backhouse & Co, 6, 9, 34-5
Green Lane, Sheffield, 5, 8, *8*
Hammond, John, 15
Hammonds (food manufacturer), 34
Harrison, William (sauce manufacturer), 14
Harvey's Sauce, 6
Havelock Square, Sheffield. 10
Hawley, Richard, 2, 36
Haxey, Lincolnshire, 3
Helders, Matt, 1
Henderson, Clara (nee Cornthwaite), 4, 10-11, *12*
Henderson, Eliza (nee Swinnerton), 10, *12*
Henderson, Henry, 2-5, 7, 9-11, *12*, 13, 27, 35
Henderson, Joseph (senior), 3
Henderson, Joseph (junior), 3
Hendogate, 1
Hinksman, Charles, x, 13, 15, 18, 20-3, *21*, 36
Hinksman, Gladys (nee Freeman), 18, 23-4, 27, 30, 36
Hinksman, Miriam (nee Shaw), 13, 18
Howard, Robert, 20
Huddersfield, West Yorkshire, 13, 18, 20, 30
Kenbourne Road, Sheffield, 10
Lea & Perrin's Worcestershire Sauce, 2, 6
Leavygreave Road, Sheffield
        Original factory at 66, 13, *17*, 20, 24
        Later factory at 41, 24, *26*, 29, 31
Low Burnham Mill, 3
McKee, Pete, 2, 33
Price, Rebecca, 5
Purnell, Webb & Co (Vinegar manufacturer), 10
Richmond, J. G., 27-30
Richmond, L, 29
Rotherham, South Yorkshire, 3, 27
Savage, Rick, 1
Shaw, George, 13, *14*
Shaw, Martin, 30

Shaw, Norman, 20
Shaw's Halifax Relish, 13
Shaws (Huddersfield) Ltd, ix, 13, *14*, 15-16, 18, 20, 30, 36
Sheffield Wholesale Grocers, 25
Skegness, Lincolnshire, 11
Spivey, Kath, 32
Steel, Mary, 23
Stoakley, E. O., 25-6
Stringfellow, Peter, 1
Thompson, Dorothy, 24
Todd, Florence (sauce manufacturer), 22
Tummon, Cecil, 15, 20, 22-3
Tummon, Malcolm, 30
Walkeringham, Nottinghamshire, 3, *4*, 11
Walster, John, 8
Waxman, Julia, vi
Webster, Simon, 32
Whitham, Rose, 15
Williams, Ada, 15
Wrigglesworth, Tom, 2
Yeomans, William (grocer and sauce manufacturer), 14
Yorkshire Relish, 6-7, 9-10, 14, 34-5, 37
Yorkshire Crisps, 37